Who Am I and Why Am I Here?

MEPHISTOPHELES.
MEANS
LIAR + DESTROYER

JANET MAYER BOOK

ALUNAYTUBE

ELITHEGODDI@gMArc.com

FRIENDS + FAMILY

Website: www.whoamiandwhyamihere.com

ISBN-13: 978-1502440983

ISBN-10: 1502440989

Cover Image:

The cover shows the sun holding the earth in its magnetic field and nicely illustrates the entire magnetic field of the earth--- an actual picture of Posi-Negativity with two forces functioning about the earth...

TABLE OF CONTENTS

1. What is God?   Page 4

2. What is Light?   Page 7

3. What is Thought?   Page 8

4. What is Holy Spirit?   Page 13

5. What is Ether?   Page 15

6. What is Soul?   Page 18

7. What is Spirit?   Page 20

8. What is Matter?   Page 21

9. What makes the moon stay in orbit?   Page 24

10. How are we born?   Page 26

11. What is Mind?   Page 29

12. Why are we here?   Page 41

13. What are Animals and Insects?   Page 51

14. What happens when we die?   Page 57

15. What are The Spheres?   Page 63

1. WHAT IS GOD?

God---meaning "Idea", or formless or unformulated Thought---came out of nothingness, only in the way the finite world defines substance. An idea is an expression by a *form* of consciousness, capable of being interpreted by the plane projecting it. Consciousness is an element. It has existence of itself apart from any other ingredient in the universe. Consciousness is *the instant of perception*, no more or no less. Idea originally came out of a condition that had nothing to do with time, space or substance. The original "idea" inside itself was not a concept in consciousness but an idea without consciousness.

Idea made itself aware of itself by becoming an introvert: by looking *into* itself and wondering what it might discover there...

God, being both cause and effect, was able to motivate idea into awareness.

God said: "Here I am, entrapped as a sort of Personage, but without any opportunity to go anywhere, or do anything, or be anything other than I am. I want expression of myself to myself, and since there is nothing outside of myself, I must get all this *within* myself. I will therefore explore myself and see how many idea divisions make me up."

God in this conception is pure and absolute subjectivity: It is the universe that is within itself; not having relationships with anything exterior to itself.

An idea does not have length, breadth, or depth: it is a thing of *philosophical concept,* not of cubic material substance. Therefore we have God originally existing as lengthless, breadthless, and depthless individuality who is blindly aware of itself as a compendium of potential Idea-Entities which, when broken up into formations of materialisms, *produced* objects having length, breadth, and depth.

God seeks some form of expression in mobile substances called Energy, so it's separate parts may have greater awareness of what constitutes the Whole, and what is *in* that Whole. Thus, it is *self-educating* insofar as its separate parts are concerned.

The Idea of the Universe is an assumption of an effect produced within itself; it is holding within itself the power to motivate itself into forms of application--- and all of it witnessable to its own perceptions!

The Universe has no bounds. It isn't a place, it's a *condition.* It's a contraption of discarnate ideas, all co-existing in the one *colossal idea;* that is, the potential creation of objects within itself. This colossal idea is not a boundable thing but all is contained in it, no matter how far the contents extend. Even Objective Space is part of its contents. In that sense, the Universe is limitless: however, *it isn't limitless when it comes to a declension of its contents* for only so many ideas make it up.

There are places within the Universe that may be ten trillion Light Years from one another: still, the cosmography of the ideas behind them is limited and, in that sense, spacial limitations occur. The Universe "runs out of ideas". When it does that, it has to come back to its original postulation of itself, which is *the whole.* It meets *itself. B*eyond that, there is no thinking.

2. WHAT IS LIGHT?

Light started in Eternal Time. Light waves are Thought Incarnate manifesting on and in substance: thus, Light has performance. If there is Light, there is Form: without Light, no form forms. God sends His Word by Light; it performs in atoms. Light is that property in ether which has the power to conceive itself in form. Light is the Word of God saying "Be" and Matter *is!* Light is the substance of Spirit performing. Light is creator of all good; it is of that substance whereby the return of spirits into earthly bodies is determined. It has vibration so fine in ether that incandescence comes---it reaches man's eyes in aspects of waves, coming to man sustaining his Spirit, making miracles happen. It goes forth into darkness, pressing Order before it. Because light vibrates, harmony makes order.

Light has the power to achieve: it goes up and down the Universe, impelling Creation before it. Even as Light brings order out of chaos, so does it impact on man's spirit and reveal its fraught Divinity. *Light makes fire, fire does not make light:* fire only kindles because light reached it.

Light is concerned in all that is; light is concerned in all that is done.

3. WHAT IS THOUGHT?

Take Substance and pull it apart and there is Energy; take Energy and pull it apart and there is Ether; Take Ether and pull it apart and there is Love; take Love and pull it apart and there is Thought; take Thought and pull it apart and there is God. Thought then is Love and Energy and Ether and Substance: these four are God because they come from God.

Thought *is,* whether Thought in raw or Thought as finished product. Thought is the basic motivation behind any earthly vehicle's manifestation. Thought *perceives* when it is aggressively reflected; it also contains "ideas". These ideas had to be manufactured: they could not exist by themselves as ideas, for ideas are not Thought, but manifestations of Thought. Ideas are the sum total of Thoughts functioning.

Acknowledging Holy Spirit's existence and conceding within the mind that its use is available, mankind realizes he has no hands with which to grasp it. We are surrounded by Holy Spirit; we are living *in* and *of* Holy Spirit; we have Holy Spirit surfeiting us, ready and faithful to be put into personal performance. Acknowledging the existence of the power brings on Holy Spirit's effects. Call upon it either blindly or intelligently, and so-called miracles result from it. And how to call upon it? The secret of it lies in *thought.*

Holy Spirit is a power vaster than that released---or releasable---in the atom bomb. Its power is available to create, to construct, to enrich, and to direct the efforts of others to actualize great social and ethical objectives. Furthermore, the phenomenon called Thought is the pipeline that enters it and brings it out stupendously. Therefore, presenting counsel on the nature and potency of Holy Spirit is truly presenting counsel on the nature and potency of *thought!*

Constructive Thought or Thought is motivated by that altruism termed love. Love is the faculty within every existing spirit to think of every manifested creation in terms of its self-improvement. Love is regard for and devotion to the interests of others. Love is the attribute that enables one to tap into the power-reservoir of Holy Spirit. Divine Love is the Father's regard for and devotion to the spiritual, and in cases, the material interests of His mortal children.

Love of itself, considered dispassionately, is both *the desire and the effort to help all other forms of life improve spiritually.* Thereby, through the immutable Laws of Compensation, one can be helped to spiritually improve. *True* Love is engaging in constructive efforts toward helping *others* make a finer and more profitable universe, and the stronger and purer it is, the less of the thought of *self* enters in.

Thought is the instrument utilized to tap into Holy Spirit. First acknowledge freely and completely in the heart that the power is available and waiting; then take the time and effort to formulate in the intellect the precise thing in every detail that is wished to be accomplished. Make this curt, clear and concise. Make it a Thought-Form and dwell upon it studiously; "concentrate on it". Suddenly, at any time during concentration upon it, the mental drill "breaks through" and the force of the energy comes gushing forth.

Remember the definition of Love when using it in connection with the tapping of Holy Spirit's power. Tap into it with a sincere desire of benefiting someone or something outside of one's self---*that* must be the sacrosanct motive. Seeking it selfishly shuts it off.

Everyone has powerful colleagues and "guides" on the upper side of the Veil, who, upon receiving these gestures of concentration, become apprised of exactly what is wished for. They bend their energies and add their resplendent efforts to see the ends materialize. It must be clear in *their* minds precisely what is wished to be accomplished: sending forth roll upon roll of crystallized Thought Forms, down to as small a detail as can be devised, until *they* unmistakably perceive it. They will concur in it and add their energies to it. Suddenly, the thing sought has been "materialized".

"Holding the thought" is not enough: "applying the thought" is a better way of depicting it. Project a great Thought-Form of what is wished for and help is effected. *The trick of the process is affecting it in altruism!*

Helping others---making them persons restored to happiness or health---creates a vacuum in which one is the creditor. One must be repaid eventually for any kindly or helpful acts, and in one's own coin: not that those others specifically may do the actual Thought Work of similar detail in return, but what is given, *must* return. Take note of that word "must". It isn't optional with Providence whether one is favored as he favored others: It's a Law of the Moral Universe that whatever is done in a loving and constructive manner *must* come back in kind. And Holy Spirit is the medium *in which and by which it happens!*

The constructive love-motive *sweeps through the cripple while he prays for his fellow sufferer,* and, more frequently than not, this cures the one who puts forth the prayer. *A healing force is a healing force,* and the person who invites it with dispassionate altruism cannot remain insensible to the presence of its benefits.

Do not interpret all of the above to imply immutable restrictions. When you find yourselves personally handicapped by a cruel condition, or become circumscribed in your efforts to aid a great labor for the enhancement of all humankind, do not think you are prohibited from tapping into the power-reservoir of Holy Spirit *yourself* because some specific person may not thereby be immediately helped. Quite the reverse is true. Sufficient concentration upon a given Thought Form, especially when you obtain the assistance of others to do it with you, can procure you anything your soul can imagine.

There is indeed a Holy Trinity: it is Spirit, Thought and Ether. Out of these three, the Universe is not only built up, it is all that is contained in whatever Universe there is. Spirit is supreme: it projects Thought on or into ether and gets materials or events as the case may be. That is the whole of creation. You are Spirit; your mental activity is Thought; the Ether is everywhere around you, waiting to be molded or directed into the results you desire. You have only to make the degree of mental effort, and *Life obeys you instead of you obeying Life!*

The power is there for the tapping. Reconstruct mental activity and focus it on Holy Spirit: send out Thought Rolls, one upon the other, and what one yearns for in wishful thinking comes unerringly to pass. Thus the existence of Holy Spirit is proven by the results it demonstrates.

4. WHAT IS HOLY SPIRIT?

Holy Spirit is *God in action!*

Holy Spirit is the primal all-pervading reservoir of Good of which the world is created, and by which the world keeps eternally functioning. It is not merciless or impersonal: it is specific, beneficent, waiting for man to reach forth and utilize it. As man does reach forth and utilize it, thereby is its existence demonstrated.

Holy Spirit's operation is a great mystery, for not only does it keep track of Karma, it also acts as the primary activating energy behind creative thought. Some names given to Holy Spirit are Primordial Force and Supernaturalism. There is a stupendous and awesome potency in it. It is a force that not only constructs and conducts the earth and universe, but also gives itself to employment and application, so mankind may do things to enrich and enhance lives of spiritual evolution.

Holy Spirit is the essential God stuff out of which the whole manifested universe is made: it is a titanic force that has only one control over it, or that responds to only one control. And that one control is Thought---altruistic Thought. Projecting or propelling sufficient Thought-Impulses into Cosmos literally controls or shapes the nature of the world and events.

Somewhere along the line of human progression it must stand reasonable to consider that certain men have arrived at a degree of spiritual understanding---or at least discovery---where they have become aware of such a Force, and grasp how to use it in performing above their fellows.

The basic God-stuff out of which Matter is built up---call it Ether, call it Love, call it what you will---always has responded to Thought, it makes no difference whether *you* propel the Thought, or if the Ancient of Days propels the Thought. You are Divine Spirit in capsule form yourselves, and Thought is Thought: the instrument by which the God-stuff is molded or diverted. The God-stuff, or basic Ether element, *does* respond to thought processes if one only employs them to the limits of strength. Instead of formulating atoms of materials, one forms patterns of behavior for oneself and one's fellows, for that is the current degree of that one's development.

Acknowledge that the whole manifested world is a *beneficent God Thought*, no matter how repellent certain aspects of it may seem. Acknowledge that the Thought Processes can be projected from one's own capsule. Divine Spirit can and will shape the pattern of behavior of those whose interests are desired to promote, *and results accrue in concrete material fact.* It is as simple as that; it is as profound as that.

Learn this truth.

5. WHAT IS ETHER?

Ether is a great and profound abstraction. Consider it as air of fine, fine substance---too fine in such substance for mortal perception.

When ether reaches a point to where it is "surcharged" with electrical processes of Thought, it "erupts", and substance called Matter is born. Matter is the combination of electrical discharges put into the ether by Thought and Vibratory Forms waiting to be filled. This activity describes the "etheric postulate:" *the essence of all created form.*

Ether is made Matter by a process of the world "going into union and coming out again," thus creating more etheric matter to an extent and duration that is infinite in its possible applications and gradations. The world "renews itself" out of reservoirs that could never become perceptible until Holy Spirit is credited as a substance---almost a *literal* substance----engaged in manufacturing Itself *out of Itself.* This is one of the mysteries of life illustrated in the phenomenon known as "procreation". The body creates young out of the physical resources of parents. Life is creating itself "out of itself," compounding and multiplying itself out of its own materials. So, too, does Holy Spirit! When this "substance" called Ether is present with thought formation to give it design, a particle called the etheric unit is born---a synchronization of original world-essence with Thought precipitation.

Matter is form perceptible to senses, yet there are also forms of Matter perceptible to senses more delicately attuned.

Thought is the primary motivator of etheric vibration. Thought and ether are two of three foundation elements that bring about physical composition. Matter doesn't think: *it is Spirit inhabiting matter that thinks!* Events are made to happen by preconceived Thought working in the element called ether to bring them about. Nothing happens that has not been "thought out" by someone, sometime, somewhere--- either incarnate or discarnate. All things happen at the behest of intensive thought. It might be a vicious thought, with vicious results: nevertheless, Thought it is: exercising in the ether to bring about a result. Nothing can *be* without Thinking first! Thought comes first; then comes fact. Thought *is!* It is the Universe "in raw". It requires no organ to manifest itself except the etheric vehicle or medium.

Matter does not think: it is Spirit that thinks---it being chiefly a form of Self-Recognizing Thought that has the distinction of identifying itself *to itself,* or to its associates.

Thought must have a vehicle by which to manifest. The essential vehicle for Spirit is called Ether. It isn't the air or the atmosphere, but the substance from which all material things are formed. Ether is "thought in raw"---all the formed or unformed Thought there is in existence, waiting to be molded by minds---celestial or mundane---into materials or behaviors, *by atomic manifestation of speeds!*

6. WHAT IS SOUL?

The soul is a shapeless and formless phenomenon of Thought *in process of self-recognition.* There is a definite rate and procedure, a definite law and order, a definite chronology of creation which determines the rate, progression, and general celerity of how the soul is born. When the manifesting God in the individual spirit-unit approaches or reaches that status of perfection that it attains to all-encompassing consciousness, through all-encompassing experience and absorption into itself of the increments from experiencing, it begins to half and quarter and split and divide and accelerate the conditions of awareness within itself to such a point that it may manifest in a thousand million units---*all in a second of worldly time if necessary!* Thus new worlds and new universes are born *ad infinitim; or cosmic families of progeny are projected that take the form of worlds or universes.*

The Life Principle is this: a soul's recognition of what part of a Divine Idea it either *is* or *can be.* Life is a protest against all other constituents who are also a part of an Absolute Whole---a sort of resentment that there can be other constituents competing with itself for recognition; and by this protest, it makes its differences known to all these other factors or material items.

There is a given rate of acceleration in consciousness, which when attained or arrived at, manifests according to a Grand Cosmic Law and, in a manner of describing it, disintegrates itself---exactly as the flywheel on a mechanical shaft can be accelerated to a point where it literally whirls itself into shattered fragments, but with *this* difference in the cosmic sense: Forever and anon in the cosmic operation, each and every fragment of the Divine Wheel immediately starts growing itself into a new wheel, with it's own rate of accelerating progress, until it has arrived at that stature and rate of progression where *it* in turn flies apart and repeats the round or cycle of generation. Thus the universe of All Consciousness whirls on and on, into constantly expanding and accelerating units of Universal Intelligence, and there is no beginning and no ending to the series of cosmic cycles that come to fruition, explode, reorganize, and grow and multiply.

Each and every fragment of this Divine Wheel is a soul that became isolated onto itself *by thinking only in terms of itself.* Then it came to recognize the existence of other similar Self-Recognizing Units (*or souls*) by experiencing their affections upon it: by knowing how they exercise their behaviors toward it and how it reacted to those experiences upon itself.

7. WHAT IS SPIRIT?

Souls or Self Recognizing Units of Consciousness were aware of themselves and others around them and needed to distinguish themselves from the other Self Recognizing Units of Consciousness.

Self-Recognizing Thought employs properties of Light to coagulate ether, Making design bodies (Light Pattern Bodies) for themselves called Spirit. Spirit is Thought operating onto itself, and proves its own identity by vehicular individuality.

Patterns for these organisms may be determined by either environment or function. Such patterns are for *purposes of identification,* as they become recognizable on their specific planes. Molecules and atoms must have some sort of design about which to group themselves so the whole may be recognized for what it is when the vehicle is complete.

8. WHAT IS MATTER?

Matter does not think.

Matter is an erroneous term. There is no such thing as matter: there is only atomic energy in forms of manifestation according to Divine Pattern. It isn't a concrete substance in universality: Matter itself is an *Idea!* It is a peculiar form of manifestation that can work its effects as another part of the *God Idea* which is witnessing the components within itself. Holy Spirit recognizes Matter as merely an instrument of itself, used for making the ego cells (which are souls) in its body know that something is setting them apart.

One can take an idea of performance and have it so volatile, or energetic of expression, that it exercises a lodestone effect on all that is around it. Manifesting this volatile expression creates motion of a sort: and of such Motion, there emerges every known substance and material known to man, manifesting in terms of what men call Light, or atomic compositions.

Matter gets its life by being made up of the same attributes as that of the Absolute Idea, as the idea manifests in a three-dimensional abstraction.

God, as an idea, is a spacial limitation of self-motivating forces, deploying within itself to get an effect. One of these effects is matter; another is individual consciousness which eventually resides in matter.

Matter is only Matter because it is something of three dimensions, and has volume and force to make an effect upon a condition of self-awareness: a condition within the Body of God by which an enhancement of awareness comes to the self-conscious cells that compose animate life.

God is seeking a way to express himself, *to* himself, in the sense of having relationships within himself and with particles making him up. These force-impellations from this self-motivating Idea deploy as two forms of exposition to get explicit results: first, it goes into the finite or material; second, it goes into the infinite as counterpoint to the finite *and becomes the so-called spiritual,* using this term to describe that which is conscious, yet intangible to materiality.

Therefore, there are two lines of evolution to follow: the Material and the Spiritual. The first is composed of tangible qualities termed Realities: that is, the *cause of sense perception* in every instance; the second is composed of intangibles who act as the benefactors from these sense perceptions. These two lines of evolution are coexistent and operate concurrently throughout the entire universe of the God-Idea body. They are labeled the Inanimate and the Animate: meaning that which is without sense perception, and that which is the recipient *from* sense perception. The universe is the God Consciousness which has the self-generating power to manifest in its parts; furthermore, one major part is *occupancy of an animate organism;* and the other major part is the *pattern that atomic energy takes* to give the phenomenon known as tangible Matter. Consciousness coagulates or shapes matter.

9. WHAT MAKES THE MOON STAY IN ORBIT?

Gravity is the *Pull* or (Positive) force coming from the earth but there are *two* forces in balance required to keep the moon in orbit: an equal and opposite, *Push* or (Negative) force that we call "Energy". Without *both* in Balance (zero), the moon would crash into the earth or fly away. Same with the sun, stars, electrons and all of the bodies in the Universe. Mathematically: $(+) + (-) = 0$ where Zero represents Balance and not "nothing" because in the world of "things" there cannot be "no-thing".

Magnetism, or 'cosmic glue,' allows each electron to move about it's nucleus, each satellite to move about it's planet, and each planet about it's sun. Each sun moves about it's centrosome---some vaster star to which it's suns are planets. Year upon year, age upon age, this orbital movement goes on. Eon follows eon, and still the circular swinging persists. Finally, all centrosomes, all Great Stars, move in their turn about the Universal Center. And there in Free Space suspends the mighty Universe, the sum-total of all moving planetary bodies, performing like clock-work, with no travel accomplished because there is nowhere to travel.

Man's motion has not been in a long line forward. Man's motion has been circular. He has moved, but always he has moved about a lodestone center. Each time in his moving, he has covered a cycle-or circle that never meets its own line in completion. Such a circle is known as a spiral. Yet man, for all his moving, for all is spiral-ascending, has been going nowhere. Where would there be a final place for him to go?

It is so with man's consciousness. Tiny God-Particles of Consciousness start out functioning, or revolving as satellites about the planet of some older and more unfolded Spirit. In time, they unfold to the dimensions of mental worlds, but even as worlds they revolve around suns. When they unfold to mammoth suns of intellects themselves---with all lesser orbs in movement around them---they swing together in spirals around the stars of Vaster Intellects.

They aren't going anywhere, they are developing! Their development is this: they are unfolding from within themselves, expanding and deploying, culturing the Great God-Consciousness that is their Vital Essence. *The secret of what is happening in great Cosmos is this:* for mortal or immortal consciousness to unfold itself, to know itself for what it is, it must operate in relation to something. It must have areas of spiritual terrain for acts of comparing itself with that which lies outside of itself, as depicted in things of form.

Conscious life is that aspect of self-recognizing observation, which proceeds to demark its own essence from the materials or objects that are not a part of it. The degree to which this recognition proceeds determines the degree or quality of the consciousness.

10. HOW ARE WE BORN?

Creation is the opposite of disruption or annihilation: it operates differently on any plane of spiritual union or universal consciousness. Birth is never cataclysmic. Birth is a progression, and progression is attainment. It manifests as a cycle about to perform for the further evaluation of the whole as perceived *within its own orbit of consciousness.*

One of the mysteries of life is the phenomenon known as *procreation:* bodies create "young" out of the physical resources of parents. Life---organic life---creates itself *out of itself.* It compounds and multiplies itself out of its own materials.

Man is born of light: Light has made him mortal. Light transcends mortal tissue and implants Spirit into embryo: cell on cell has grown because of it, resulting in physical organisms.

Organisms are the material enhousements for Electing Units of Self-Recognizing Consciousness. These organisms are capable of obeying the dictates of the enhoused Consciousness, so Consciousness can get action and motion. It is Self-Recognizing Thought directing the animate assembly while inhabiting it.

Organisms are first physical bodies which get vehicular effect on the plane of materialism. Second, the Light Pattern Bodies give physical bodies their shape, size and biologic design; and third, the unit of Self-Recognizing Consciousness dwells in the pineal gland of organic brain. The pineal and pituitary glands contain all the ingredients consciousness will ever need to use while in its earthly body. They contain them in their full-blown essence from the instant the psyche enters the physical body, or its brain habitation...

Soul employs properties of Light to make Design Bodies for itself. These Design Bodies provide tracks for material atoms to follow: thereby building a structure that serves Thoughts desire for spiritual mobility. Thus, Soul can command Light Forces. The Light Forces thus having been requisitioned and brought into Pattern, establish a blueprint for uniform assembly of material atoms. A field of Magnetic Force is set up to attract material atoms, so the totality of them in operation becomes observable as a Body and for all practical purposes operates as a Body.

A Body---a living body---is nothing but a *light pattern* shaped by soul which attracts atoms to such a degree that solidarity results. Soul controls the atomic body after first controlling or creating the Light Body. *Soul is a deathless unit!* It has never had a formal design onto itself: it shapes etheric form by copying the accredited presentation for a material body.

A soul settles upon who its parents are to be. Having seen its prospective parents "take off" from the spiritual realm to be earthly people in advance of it, it marks the time until it is to join them physically as their infant. That soul will probably remain spiritually close to those who are to be its forthcoming parents: it will watch them through their own childhood and adolescences, and perhaps even go so far as to assist them in meeting and mating. Marriage results on schedule as it was planned between all of them twenty to thirty solar years before, and presently the wife-mother is expecting. Then the soul knows its own moment is approaching when it is due to relinquish free spirithood. It gets the electrical rate of vibration of that embryo or fetus and transfers it's consciousness into it for a predetermined number of years of residence.

The instant the Soul Consciousness ceases to exercise in the etheric Light Body (because it has "gone to sleep" in its new mother's womb) the vibrations that moments ago made its old Light Body a tangible thing, die away. So, for all intents and purposes, it ceases to have an identity. Subsequently, it will awaken to a new sense of itself in its fresh infantile envelope of flesh, and begin the tried and proved process of creating a new Light Pattern Body to distinguish its new career. It will continue to operate in this new Light Body until some moment, scores or hundreds of years hence, it finds itself repeating the same cycle of birth and death and birth again, as it has done literally hundreds of times already.

11. WHAT IS MIND?

Mind acts as a communications link between the Pineal and Pituitary glands. The individual life, when translated down into the Particle designed for adjustment within the mortal organism, is an Essence of God, and might be termed the Spirit-Ego, called the Spirit God-Man, who should always be in control of the physical vehicle, no matter how that vehicle is used to gain experience.

The Spirit God-Man must have an instrument for executing its commands to the physical body, as well as an instrument for receiving the educational sense perceptions in counteraction, so it can absorb them into its psyche. That vehicle is *Mind.* Mind is not a thing unto itself like the Spirit God-Man or the physical body: it acts as the *bridge-cap* between the two sides and partakes of the properties of both. Just as a bridge has its abutments secured on either side of the river's banks, without the river's banks, it has no identity as a bridge. Mind is the bridge between the Little Spark of Divine Consciousness, which should command all actionable behaviors in one's life, and the physical vehicle; it is through the physical vehicle that the Divine Spark attains education from its sense perceptions.

Mind does not have anything to do with the operations of the brain, except when Mind utilizes brain as a physical instrument: either to initiate physical actions to express its command, or to receive information from its receptivities. Brain is a purely physical organ; geographically speaking, it is the Seat of Consciousness to the individual because it encases the Pineal and Pituitary gland. These glands serve as Master-Nerve Ganglia by sending and receiving impulses to and from any point of the physical compass.

The brain is a definite physical organism and a component part of the purely physical assembly, as the hand or foot, quite as useful and quite as useless after the Spirit God-Man terminates his educational experience in the mortal sheathing. Brain is the sole instrument of Spirit and Mind for getting their physical demands executed.

In the Pineal Gland there is an instrument of perception, a Voice Structure. The voice from this structure travels back and forth between the pineal sense of consciousness, which is the Spirit God-Man in sentient activity, and the various departments of the physical brain. This Voice Structure describes Mind as a bridge-thing. A voice *as* a voice is a series of sounds performing the function of transferring symbols of speech. Mind does not do this: it is in a sense the speech itself, buried and operating within the confines of the physical brain. Mind cannot be entrapped in any other vehicle than organic brain, although it can operate in Pure Karma. It can operate at the behest of the Spirit God-Man in finer vehicles of etheric substance, almost to infinity: there, it informs the God Man Consciousness of the happenings of the etheric events external to itself. Brain always has to act as the physical agent of the physical members.

Spirit and Body are understandable as separate entities; and the connecting link between them requires much elucidation, especially when considering the subject of ill-health.

Mind is Mind, unqualified and unqualifiable: the bridge-cap between the Spirit and the physical assembly. It may have declensions of activity but it is the same resolute factor at all times and performs only one function: apprising the Spirit of what is going on around it, and of things affecting its mortal habitat, wherever that happens to be.

Mind cannot function by itself except in extraordinary cases. It is a sort of consciousness-torturer, afflicting consciousness with a sense of its own reality while in the physical encasement. *Mind is a galvanizing force.* Think of mind as a concrete thing, perhaps in terms of the electric spark playing between the elements of a spark plug in a gas engine. The spark appears to be a thing in itself: a substance of fire, traveling back and forth between the elements; it can even be photographed like material objects.

Mind is not literally the spark, any more than the spark in a gas engine is the electricity responsible for the ignition: the spark in the latter case is the *externalized evidence* that the electric state is present. Likewise, this Voice of Consciousness, or the articulateness that is within the brain---aware or unaware of itself as such---is evidence of the Mind State functioning externally. And just as electricity cannot be drawn as a picture---because it is an etheric condition called the Magnetic Field in operation---a picture cannot be drawn of Mind. Nevertheless, Mind is a potent and tangible thing.

Normally, Mind does not intrude itself into physical employments until it is invited by causes from outside itself, just as electricity does not ordinarily intrude itself into the function of physical objects, one with another, until there is an absence of equilibrium in etheric conditions, or until some sort of materialistic formulation invites it. These formulations are secured according to principles known as Laws, and in this regard, Mind is also subservient to Laws of Operation The difference between *electrical laws* of harmony, and *mental laws* of harmony is this: the electrical is impersonal in its operations or control, whereas the mental is at the direction of the conscious spirit-ego and responsive to it throughout every instance of sentient life in the body.

The *mental* life is not a thing apart from the *spiritual---*though both can be something apart from the physical. The laws operating the Mind are always for the *guidance of the spiritual.* They are called 'laws', exactly as displays of electrical energy are defined by terms of formula, because even under the control of Spirit, certain conditions have to be paramount in excellence before Mind can proceed with its functioning. These conditions of excellence are universally the same in all animate creatures. The only difference is in their *effect,* since the construction of each creature has its own intricate composition---it contains its specific receptivities to cause personal awareness from advanced forms of stimuli.

Electrical energy moves in a field of force called the magnetic area: it has *current*---an angle of movement or direction of application. The thing known as Mind lacks this qualification. It operates without regard to visual effects. Mind is not diagramable in the sense of an electric current: it operates a living *condition,* which is its own field of force. Thus the phenomenon of *etheric vibration.*

Mind is an intermediary between Ego and Brain that has properties and functions of its own, which crystallizes in employment foreign to each, and therefore may be accepted as a separate and independent thing. It is subject to the whims and caprices of its master, the divine Spirit Essence that is the sentient soul, yet it may also sometimes rebel against that essence or soul.

In Animate Nature there are three factors: Spirit-Soul, Mind, and the Physical Organism that includes the brain. The Spirit-Soul is the God-Presence in the human assembly, or the mortally conscious state. Then, there must be an instrument by which the Divine Essence utters it's fiats to the physical assembly and receives repercussions therefrom, thereby constituting and manifesting the mortal state of awareness. *That instrument is Mind.* It is self-sufficient as long as the other two factors of the equation are in equilibrium with it. However, there is turmoil the moment one of them ceases to function in balance.

Turmoil of this order is Disease and Malady. When this turmoil approximates a state where Mind is so out of balance with either it's Soul-Spirit or it's Physical

Assembly, in such a way where coordination can never be regained, death results instantly. That *is* physical death. Spirit goes on about its business, taking Mind with it as a recalcitrant administrator, to give it a fresh opportunity for administration under a new set of conditions where former tumults are negligible.

Under ordinary conditions, when Spirit has a motive to execute in physicality, the Spirit-Ego becomes aware that it should do something for a spiritual reason: as in an act relating to the adjustment of its Karma. It then knows the body must go through certain pleasure-pain sensations to effect this experience, which then works it's compensation on the Ego's consciousness.

The Spirit-Ego says to the Mind "tell the brain to perform so-and-so". Whereupon the Mind, being the agent of Spirit, says to brain, "Do so-and-so". The brain in turn, picks up the message and attempts to translate it in terms of behavior. Perhaps it encounters an obstruction in the physical sense: the nerves and organs may not possess sufficient vitality to effect performance; or the cost in energy may be too great; or the obstruction may be a lack of concrete physical endowment such as a crippled limb brought about by external accident---this handicapping execution---or, there may be a condition within the body over which the brain cannot exercise control due to short-circuits or paralysis of nerve fibers. Many conditions may maintain that keep brain and body from performing.

Nevertheless, Spirit continues to insist that the performance be executed, and at once Mind rises up like the angry servant it is and speaks to its master saying, "I'm telling you the minions under me are impotent to work your will, yet I have no recourse but to bear the brunt of your displeasure that this is so. I will try to do what I can for you: I will strive for the nearest results approximating what you want done, or the condition you want effected". Mind begins to work while carrying a sort of disgruntlement between its commander and the captain of the forces under him. This results in alienating the two forces, which in time works open combat. Mind is out of sympathy with its unreasonable commander; it is disgruntled and does one of two things: it either functions synthetically by bringing about a wholly different result than what is wanted, or it says to Spirit, "Command your own functionaries, for you have made my offices intolerable". This latter postulate is known as insanity or utter idiocy.

When Mind is overtaxed by implausible commandments, so functioning is impossible in the normal way, there is either a rebellion on the part of Mind or Mind quits altogether and does not seem to manifest. The latter status is usually brought about by either congenital weakness or physical accident to the brain.

Disease is a condition where there is improper coordination between Spirit, Mind, and Physical Equipment.

Mind apprises the Spirit of conditions maintaining within the body, as well as operates the body at the behest of Spirit; but Spirit will not listen if it chooses not to listen. Mind listens within itself, and looks to its eagerness---or anxiety---to work out its destiny in the quickest possible order. Yet when regarding the beginning of ill-health, *Spirit is the arch offender* in each instance: it is selfish, obtrusive, arrogant, and dominant: it says to the physical assembly in material exposition, "You are my slave to do with as I will: obey me or I will destroy you." The poor physical equipment finds itself faced with a necessity of 'making bricks without straw to please Pharaoh'.

When the Spirit is thus unreasonable, and yet persists in its driving force for obedience, something has to give. Either Mind collapses and goes quiescent, or it works abortively and introduces physical derangement among the bodily factors, accomplishing purposes that have no bearing on the original commands.

This is what happens with Disease in the physical assembly: Man catches a cold or develops a germ that, over a period of time, malforms his organs. Attacking the vital organs, the condition assumes a stage where the malformation is so great that Mind is unable to redirect the vital forces galvanizing the members to efficient activity. The man dies, not through corrosion of the vitals, but because Spirit and Mind do not coordinate; they do not endeavor to restore the lost balance by setting up conditions where a reasonable amount of harmony can exist among all three entities.

Spirit has the chance to organize itself in relation to Mind and Body, that Mind always has control over the physical members at the harmonious stipulations of Spirit. The time will come when this will be so generally conceded and observed *that humankind will be able to prolong physical life to any extent that it chooses.* In these instances, it is Spirit who is stupidly exacting because Spirit does not fully understand the possibilities and impossibilities of the physical vehicle that is supplying it with experience. Mankind's problem is to learn how to correlate the three components to the efficient experiencing of life in the flesh.

Individual Spirit behaves badly, or does not behave at all, and it is constantly short-suiting itself in the very things it is most eager to acquire: nominal experience. It wants to acquire knowledge derived by contact with occupancy of matter. In no case can Spirit retract what it has commanded if those commandments had been too implausible of execution or too inane of concept for the Mind-Brain to carry out. Death must release the particle of foolish consciousness, and let it enter into another vehicle at some other time to learn the process, and the practice of the process with greater efficiency.

Individual Spirit is not always willing to recognize what Death is about. It obeys blind forces, and therefore issues equally frenzied and purblind orders to its minions. Furthermore, since mind is not free to adjudge itself in its inherent activities, the turmoil becomes great and piteous. Spirit wants to obey the exactions of its Karma, but sometimes with such vitalities that it overlooks the equal exaction of its flesh and thus drives the physical vehicle to almost criminal extremes.

One drives one's body to extremes by 'will power', or the infusion of drugs, until a state is reached where the body is utterly out of control from the mind. One tries to lift his hand but finds it is paralyzed: he has paralyzed it. Consequently, there is no willful control over the physical assembly, for Mind has suspended. One could keep this up, if he were so foolish, until the heart failed or the brain burst a blood vessel and death occurred.

More often, the mind is not entirely in that state of lassitude where it is unable to function, and it calls for a succession of bodily effort by thrusting a barrier of sleep---the equivalent of death in a lesser mode---between the spirit eager to perform, and the devitalized body unable to respond. Mind is now acting in defiance of its commander, with a certain individuality of its own, which would seem to make it a separate personality. It isn't that, else we would have two people residing in the same physical equipment. Rather, it is Personality operating without Ego.

The mind 'short-cuts' itself and acts at the behest of higher laws, or increments of intelligence, than those commanded by the Spirit Ego. It ceases to be commanded by the Spirit Ego, (which is the individual will), and looks to the Great Over-Soul of Humanity for its commanding. Mind is now ruled by the phenomenon of Thought Incarnate, or that Essence from which the soul first came as an individual particle of consciousness.

Mind itself has no individuality, it has an organism that is sensitive to intelligence and responds to it. When the Soul is negligent, Mind vacates its offices and yields control to the higher intelligence that originally gave it birth as a functioning unit. Therefore, the phenomenon of *laws in the higher intelligence* is securing a response from sentient Mind---which is the instrument for carrying out the dictates of consciousness---and thereby reverting to results called instincts. There may be conditions postulated where the Mind itself becomes unable to turn to those Higher Potentialities because there is no fundamental law covering the specific case, there is then a mental breakdown, or permanent cessation of any physical functions.

The man who constantly and continually overworks and flagellates himself until his coordination is completely in chaos, is committing a certain kind of suicide. It is Spirit that is deficient in knowledge about the extremities of the physical vehicle, and about the factors operating the mental vehicle under it. These can be correlated for a perfect performance, so physical suffering or ultimately demise may never need to be.

Death is the acme and apex of that quality in the human system called Disease, as it manifests it's disarrangements and all the factors motivating it. This is not a banality, because it says *Death may be conquered by knowledge of the principals involved,* by having Spirit direct the Mind intelligently and reasonably; without a sense of strain derived from over taxation. A good percentage of distressful fatigue is due to *mental conflict.* A strain exists between the driving power of the externalized idea that says completion is necessary, and a sense of awareness that completion is still in the future and may never be consummated.

There is no physical malady that cannot be cured by the proper correlation of spiritual dictates and mental responses so there would never need be such a thing as ill-health in the universe. Disease is Dis-Ease, not of bodily function but of mental endowment in juxtaposition over bodily functions. Therefore, command the body as a loving lord who sympathetically gives orders to a beloved servant and three-quarters of the human maladies will vanish overnight...

12. WHY ARE WE HERE?

Life in Cosmos has one single intent, one single purpose, one single message, one single meaning, one single attribute and one single wholesomeness; *it is self-awareness.* Heightened self-awareness is the crucial point that is operating behind the universe's facade.

The sum and substance of all life is to make it know *that it is*, then *what it is*, then *what it can become.* The purpose of existence for each is to first know experience; then to grasp the full possibilities and potentialities *in* existence; so, in the course of time, the individual consciousness attains to *Cosmic Consciousness* or The Absolute.

There are three great classifications of souls living in earth-life, with each soul manifesting a life plan in their particular division. Each division serves a definite purpose. The first classification comprises all those who came into life to get earthly experiences in their own right, and for their soul's profit. This great grouping includes practically half of all living persons on the planet: it takes in that great army of ordinary folk whose lives are made up of constant change: upset and alternate adventures of grief and happiness, or turmoil and tranquility. They are in mortal bodies and going through life adventures so they can "speak from experience" in any given capacity or role. From each adventure and experience they get something that remains in their character---*something they need---*

although often they do not fully appreciate that they have needed it. They little realize how much their experiencing has contributed to their character-building.

The second classification of souls on earth, in point of numbers, comprises all those who came to life to perform some special service toward a given individual or group that they have been involved with in other lives they have lived.

The third classification of souls on earth, comprising a much smaller number, includes a group of what we might call "Master Souls". They have no special personal or family reasons for coming into life because they have long since perfected themselves in character; therefore, earthly return does not supply them with as much profit as they could obtain in higher manifestations of spiritual life. They make their descent into flesh in order to minister to the race or to society as a whole. This class takes in almost all the great leaders of each race---in science, art, diplomacy and religion: all those who work with a mysterious selflessness for the good of humanity as a whole.

Accomplishing these three purposes involves profound factors. Years of study are required to perfect a knowledge of just why life is what it is in each individual instance and what each soul needs to acquire by going into it. This means people in the great mass of Pure Thought---if they are advanced and balanced persons---take long periods before reincarnating to digest the necessities and requirements of their own peculiar characters. After having arrived at decisions as to what they still require, they take even longer periods for studying and determining the time and manner in which they will go down into new physical bodies for further earthly sojourns.

They never rush into life promiscuously or carelessly, or in a moment of caprice. The factors attending the life process are by no means insignificant. In the higher and finer arenas of etheric life there are persons with great mental endowments and spiritual foresight: these act as guides and mentors by helping souls who sincerely desire a quick return into the earthly classroom; they can find the times and means for quickly bringing about such re-entrances. These personages are the great "soothsayers" of opportunity: they are the wise ones of Cosmos who know human life and its strange behavior-complexes. They have a bird's-eye-view of the race, so to speak, knowing what will probably result from given factors in any given life-proposal. They have a foreknowledge of, or can figure out in advance, what human attributes and opportunities will give the soul seeking entrance *real life probabilities* to obtain what it is striving to acquire.

For example, if a soul wants to revisit earthly life to become a little stronger in the attribute of patience, it would scarcely seek normal, well-poised and flawlessly moral persons to act as its father and mother. To comply with conditions necessary for a soul's growth in patience, the parents ought rather to be small-minded, mean-spirited and highly-excitable in their daily adjustments towards each other. They should generally conduct themselves as hotboxes of temper and be fighting most of the time: plaguing and tormenting the child out of its growth for no other reason than to vent their own spleens.

It would be astonishing to know how many people choose parents whose incompatibilities will teach them patience. This is to provoke the child, and make it mad with envy of the parent's power to act so unilaterally. They provoke the child into having certain features of character, which necessitates in its own turn, self-control in its own right. Uniformly, parents are chosen who are so rambunctious at times, and constitute such an everlasting thorn in the child's mental peace, that the child slowly begins to covenant within itself to not make a similar show of itself to others; rather, it will become an improvement on the dispositions of father and mother. Thus, the entrant-soul will learn in practice the life lesson they sought.

Patience is one of the prime lessons behind a soul's reentry into the earthly classroom, and there is good reason for this that should never be ignored. Lack of patience disturbs universal order by shooting the soul forward in spiritual progress faster than it is equipped to go. The soul needs to learn that it can only make progress *after* it is well-rounded in *all* the fundamentals that go into making up its existence as the "thinking machine" each person essentially is. However, the impatient soul sees others journeying into higher planes of Order and Love and obtaining spiritual attributes; it sees these attributes manifesting in those advanced characters and wants to be like them, without stopping to recognize exactly what makes them what they are. It wants to take a short-cut to attainment, but if it were allowed to do this, it would soon find itself at a pathetic loss.

Only what's known to stay known can profit the spirit, and what's known to stay known can only be gained by experiences of the highest and deepest quality. Furthermore, this Celestial Education requires the Soul-Spirit to keep up the cosmic tempo within its own individuality: it must follow orderly processes and not go shooting off at tangents out of envy or malice, or because the opportunity seems to beckon. Patience keeps one in balance by making the soul attain through its specific instrument and within its proper media, without disgruntlement or malice.

There are other lessons the soul learns while in life, even though the primary requisite may be the need for patience. It may learn to have love for others, and to have consideration for the rights of weaker persons. It may learn the necessity for being gentle, for being polite, and for deploring and avoiding hatred: verily a score of minor attributes that go into making up the well-balanced person. Nevertheless, whatever the lesson may be, when you see a child getting its education by being more or less knocked around and abused by short-tempered parents, do not get maudlin over it, or think the Almighty is very cruel to the tot for putting it under the power of such unpleasant people. The Almighty had practically nothing to do with it except to create children and parents and put them into a chosen environment. Then they are left to evolve spiritually through their contacts with each other. Such a child unerringly *chose* those parents by its own volition because it specifically wanted what those parents had to give it.

Birth in no instance happens by chance, and no child ever has parents it did not choose in advance. Of course, *this is by no means an argument for the abuse of children,* or the persecution of weak intellects who are not able to withstand too rigorous a training in specific mortal doses. If matters get beyond the point of the child profiting from its situations, to where it is being *damaged spiritually* instead of helped, Cosmos usually takes care of it by having the child meet with some sort of accident or it contracts some malady that lifts it back upon Planes of Spirit: then it gets a fresh start under better circumstances, where measures of iniquity will be meted out more sparingly.

To say uniformly that every child everywhere is getting approximately the treatment it deserves from any pair of parents, under any and all conditions, is to speak a vital truth bluntly and completely. However, it does not follow that the child consciously knows in every instance exactly what is coming to them: 'factors and trends' are the known qualities by which a coming life-path is evaluated. Nevertheless, given those factors and trends in the parental combination, the lessons---bitter or otherwise---are usually gone through with for better or for worse.

There are a lot of emotional people running around the planet saying, "Children should be treated as 'Little Souls fresh from the lap of God'". Some of those coddled souls may be hoary with age. They may be persons who have been the most despicable tyrants and criminals in other dispensations, and utterly reprehensible people in their social contacts. Or they may be persons who are motionless in seas of lost opportunities for spiritual profit, who have taken physical form for no other reason than to truly get the treatment they know they will get under the parents they have selected or in the environment in which we find them living. Whether born in city slums or mountain shack, in Orient or Occident, amid wealth or squalor, the child has selected that locale by its own volition.

Life might be a far different thing on earth today if mediocre parents by the thousands could truthfully become aware of the past identities of the 'child souls' they put to bed every night---with every consideration given to them for their welfare, which indeed they merit---when all the time those children may be ages older than the parents who show them such solicitude. No matter what the circumstance in which a child is being reared, there are good and sufficient reasons for that child's environment of the moment. The chances are ten to one, if the mission is going astray or the lesson is not being learned, that the child will 'die' by sickness or accident before it reaches maturity.

Take the case of a child who has come into life to learn the aforesaid lesson of patience. It gets itself born to irascible parents; it grows up a normal child with normal reactions to parental incompatibility, and finally gains from an exact realization of the utter uselessness of its being cantankerous in its personal desires and demands upon society. It is intimidated because its bombastic spirit meets with rebuffs at every turn: it's proclivities toward too much independence are turned inward upon itself, and this manifests as a form of self-pity. A new factor has arisen in this individual's life outside of the need of patience: it has to learn emotional control, or the ability to keep a balanced viewpoint in the face of adversity, hardship and rebuff. It has to learn to stroke forward without undue thought to its own principles of conscience, or bogus and silly estimates of its own worth to Cosmos. Thus, out of one lesson grow others: scorn for the seeming dictates of circumstance; steadiness confronting a lying environment and all the thousand and one deceptions that attempt to bewilder and delay the soul's progression through life.

With this first classification of people---those periodic visitors into mortality for purposes of self-profit---it shouldn't be difficult to see why the other two classifications become of moment. Time and time again, this thing happens: while the soul is living in the first classification, obtaining profits for itself alone, it incurs obligations for some great service rendered to it; or it does some dastardly thing that temporarily injures another soul in its development and creates a situation that has to be adjusted in kind. In other words, the souls have to go back into life and go through a repetition of the relationship, or at least enter into a relationship whereby the debt may be liquidated.

As for those qualified souls who come down into life to serve the race as artists, teachers, men of science or civic leaders: such classification is obvious in its essence. The point to be considered is that each is in life serving one of three motives. Just which motive a soul is serving is not so important to know at present as it is to have the enlightenment that a motive is being served and if he were not doing it with a reasonable amount of success, he would not continue in life for any length of time.

In respect to parents, they uniformly ought to be held blameless for whatever their natural and instinctive attitudes may have been toward the child, for they will be giving the child what it solicited. Children may be expected to conform to the trainings and adjurations of the parents, but the parents are under no obligation to conform to the trainings and adjurations of the children. Parents live their own lives and work out their own karmas, one toward the other: the children behold the situations thus created and desired participation in them. Having accepted life under such conditions, they should have no complaints to make against their parents for the type of home they provided them, or for the things the parents have done for them or not done for them. If the parents are callous or even brutal toward a child, it is well to view the matter with as much philosophy as possible by making the allowance that very probably such treatment has been wanted by the child-soul so it might develop Self-Reliance.

What the individual child's needs may be in every instance---which causes it to enter life through the parents it possesses---is not the important thing to know: that would require listing as many answers as there are children and parents. The principle to be retained and the enlightenment to be appreciated is the fact that spiritual increment is being expected and received. As one grows in general knowledge of cosmic operating's about such matters, understanding will deepen: then, when flagrant cases of eccentric relationships are beheld between children and parents, one can look more and more *behind* the mere physical situation and speculate on the *cosmic* gains that are doubtlessly being delivered.

The soul needs to learn that it can only make progress *after* it is well rounded in *all* the fundamentals that go into making up its existence as the "thinking machine" each person essentially is.

13. WHAT ARE ANIMALS AND INSECTS?

Biologists consider the indigenous earthly orders as various species that came into being by chance or lucky accident. They advance the theory that environment and natural selection have been responsible for the million and one species that have had existence on the earth. The question is asked: "Why are these creatures acting so and how did they become what they are?" A strange species appears in life, or a plant is discovered blossoming afar in a desert place and it is unquestioningly accepted as natural phenomena. Thus the term "Nature" describing something that creates oddities without apparent cause.

Consider a certain species of tree with the trait of encasing its seeds in tiny swirls of cobwebby fluff, which the passing wind tears from its mother pod so they can waft across far landscapes, giving its seedlings maximum circulation. Does that tree have thinking and logical intellect to provide transportation for its seedlings? Or consider the breed of wasp who will lay her eggs in the nest she has fabricated, and then go to find a certain kind of caterpillar, which she proceeds to sting in a vital place to paralyze it. Afterwards, she transports it to her nest and seals it up with her young, knowing her own hours of life are limited for having spawned them. Are such discernments for providing the young larvae with nourishment arising from her own mental processes? Doesn't such intelligence indicate a quality of consciousness high above an insect? Lower orders of life in the natural world have profounder wits that do their thinking for them.

Upon lofty octaves of intelligence, intellects are manifesting who make it their business to act as counselors to their spirit detachment or to those paths that given groups of self-conscious entities pursue, so those spirits may expand and increase their conscious awareness. They are not creators so much as Prescribers for Creations. They are a high, high order of scientists experimenting with earth's biological forms, only instead of striving to arrive at the fabrication of products by combining chemicals as earthly scientists do, they have in view circumspectly *the enhancement of consciousness in individualistic organisms*---in which the Item of Limitation and its profits are forever of consequence.

These majestic Prescribers of Creation are the designers of the million-and-one orders of life that constantly appear and disappear from various planets. They try them out and test them; they observe tangible effects upon the individual units of consciousness who are occupying these various forms of life. They remark upon these effects that come from each organism's specifically assigned limitations to the consciousness that would make its progress in that organism. They supply and define the lesson-capabilities pertinent to each species.

Nothing appears anywhere in Cosmos without a *cause;* and nothing assumes a given shape, or activates in a given function without its fecundities and ramifications having been designed by a Master Brain. Profounder wits are very real and decidedly active. Prescribers of Creation are the carpenters and mechanics of the natural universe. In them and behind, them a stupendous purpose is being served: they are finding a million and one ways for Consciousness to develop itself by entering into and exercising certain forms, and then combining the features of those forms over interminable periods so the best things propagate. *Self-Conscious Life* partakes of the same essence irrespective of the form; however the limitations or peculiarities of the form work different effects on consciousness by intensifying it or enhancing it according to its peculiarities.

For instance, the honeybee cultivates it's consciousness in a manner that would never accrue to an elephant. The mosquito singing so annoyingly in the night does not extract a different value out of its structural aliveness than the worm in the apple or the dolphin besporting in the course of a ship. Is Consciousness, as consciousness, any different between them? A purpose is being served in each, and the purpose aimed at distinguishes the form or the features of the species. The unit of self-awareness does not vary as self-awareness, only in its vehicle of expression.

All life has its right to exist and work out its own destiny. *All Life is Life,* with Holy Spirit making it the phenomenon it is. The order of reincarnation from living form to living form is inexorably upward. Retrograde is dissolution and it is always the *individual form* that perishes, not the life-particle as a phenomenon in itself.

Nothing exists in the finite world that is not the product of a deliberate Thought manifesting. *Deliberate thought never manifests lacking a worthy purpose.* Nothing exists in the finite world that does not serve some practical kind of profitable relationship to something else. These practical capacities may conflict with one another, and the gain of one may be the loss of another, at least when temporarily considered, but they always serve the Purpose for which they were designed and projected. The louse, cockroach, termite, rattlesnake, or even the predatory tiger may be inimical to man's purpose in manifesting as man, but none of these is inimical to those creatures as themselves. *The Cross-annoyance* is one species over and against another species, and is only regarded as annoyance by the more advanced aspects of Manifesting Consciousness who forgets that antagonism is merely one of contrast.

The fundamental nature of instincts in the species vehicle manifests as it's *prescriptions for conduct while it moves on earth,* with these being agreed to beforehand by the entity who would embody themselves in that organism. These seek spiritual gains from confinement in certain peculiar forms. The great hierarchy of Prescribing Creators, whose function in the universe is to find more facile ways for units of Consciousness to improve their expansions in

Self-Awareness, is the "brooding oversouls" of each species in each instance.

The Oversoul, also called the Group Spirit, perceives it's carefully equipped species coming into successful issue and sees the species' intelligence increasing to where individualized units begin to assume character or personality. This frequently happens for instance in a highly bred horse or dog. Even though it exists in the bodily organism of an animal, it's intellect seems almost human. This trait of Consciousness is performed by all sentient creatures on all octaves of Consciousness-progression.

A person's capability to evaluate a lower species of intelligence is indicative of a certain attainment in his own right. That person perceives in them his own lessons learned, from his own long habitations in organic housings of a certain species: these have become so well learned in both, that they almost function automatically. They have been incorporated in that person's character and become an automatic display of that person's particular unit of *consciousness in action.* All of it is Memory, for Character and Memory are inseparable. Each is a feature of the other: they are polarities of the one phenomenon of self-awareness.

The ability to be aware of *self* is evidence of activation by Holy Spirit itself. Such activation takes many forms up through many aeons. Each form is working out its own purpose solely to benefit the self-awareness housed inside it. There is a Oneness to *all* self-manifesting life, based upon this root cause of all sentient behavior. And while different forms may cross in activities, or become antagonistic to each other as forms---even preying upon each other as food for self-preservation against hunger---*the Law of the Process operates for the perpetuation of the form*, and this to profit the self-aware unit inside it. Each form has its integrity unto itself and the license to preserve itself at the expense of another form. It may not succeed in doing this, but even if it loses the contest, the enhoused spirit-germ or consciousness unit still profits. Learning specific agilities to escape from hazards is one of the major educators and developers of Spirit consciousness since it enhances itself in its self-realizations.

14. WHAT HAPPENS WHEN WE DIE?

"Finer forms of ether" fill the spaces between the atoms and molecules of Matter perceptible to mortals. Within these atoms and molecules of finer substances are still other atoms and molecules more finely perceptible. In that observation is the secret clue as to "where we go when we die". These finer vibrations and compositions interpenetrate and exist in the same dimensions as material concepts of reality---a realm of reality that interpenetrates actual molecules and atoms. This world of reality exists within the atomic spaces of bodies and materials. There are terrific empty spaces within each and every atom of the material world: the distances between protons and electrons are stupendous; rearing actual structures of still finer atomic substances *within* those distances.

When the physical self lies in deep sleep at night, the etheric body gently floats inertly six to fifteen inches above the prostrate physical form. This maintains regardless of the posture of the physical form on its bed. If suddenly awakened, the Etheric figure will whip electrically back into the physical form and that form will appear to be fully "aroused". There is a cable connection between the torso of the one and the torso of the other in the area called the solar plexus. There is also a perfect Spanish-moss nest of fibers between the cranium of one and the cranium of the other. Upon death the main "cable", not more than ten to fifteen inches long, comes out of the breast of the dying individual and enters into the etheric counterpart slightly below the shoulder-blades of the figure "hovering" over him. This cable is about the thickness of a finger and is greyish-purple in color. When it breaks, the separation happens close to the etheric shoulder-blades. Then the tangled web of head-strands parts. The heart ceases beating electrically with the breaking of the "cords". The dying individual will perceive several presences arriving to conduct the soul-spirit to the Thought Plane on which it belongs.

The cable, or Silver Cord, is not a material thing made of material substance. It is composed of Ether similar to the "material" of the Pattern Body in which the subconscious intelligence resides. It can pass without difficulty through solid walls and meteorological conditions have no effect on it. It partakes of the "substance" of a Thought Beam or the character of a radio wave, both of which have an affinity to light.

Upon death, the Silver Cord connecting the Physical self and the Etheric self has been severed. The instant that there is a break between the physical and etheric mechanisms by reason of disconnection of this "life-cord", every physical animation ceases at once. By no means, however, does etheric animation likewise cease, because it is the etheric that supplies the life-force to the correal. The Etheric is self-sustaining, the physical is not. It is the presence of the Etheric Self in, or attachments of the Etheric self to, the body that keeps it animate and functioning.

There is neither pain nor distress in death as a

phenomenon. Death in itself is painless. Not only is it painless, it may be a sensual delight to many who have been living their lives in physical distress. It's a *relief* to such people: a personal escape from the pain and distress of their wracked organisms.

When the transition is being made, the first sensation will be for one to know he is "dying; it may even feel like "silken threads are snapping". One lets go of muscles and organs, never to resume them again in that specific body. One may have the sensation of "going down" because of the incapability of controlling past physical reflexes. Everything is cutting loose and giving freedom---absolute freedom of mental perception. It may become overwhelming--- one may be "lost" in the first fearsome rush of it. The consequence is that one "blanks himself out" until finding himself anew by a unique and peculiar process. This process has to do with the nearest and dearest who have made the ascent: and one will be called into a truer realization of oneself by spoken implorings from his family of loved ones, or by those who have come to take him in custody.

No one comes to die without these higher dimensions of thought being aware of his coming over in advance. The death-state is known as positively as the occurrence of the equinoctial year, for it is written in each astronomical Karma. The dear ones know the exact date and moment when one is expected to make the transition. Each has arranged it himself before coming into flesh, saying: "I will exist in mortal organism from this date to that date". And, it is kept religiously, because if it isn't kept it would upset the sternest phases of the Karmas of others---as in the case of suicide.

An exact date of return to the thought plane is set and it is kept, because enhousing and enwrapping circumstance sees to it that it is kept. The Death Circumstance is the expectation of others in the higher phases of life that one will make one's reappearance among them at a given "pass point" in cosmic happenings---and they rely upon it because they know they *can* rely upon it. One will hear "voices of thought speech" from those who preceeded him unto the thought planes: they will be present with him, to take charge when the "silken threads snap" so no mental harm accrues while psychically "unconscious".

Nine out of ten will probably die in their beds, not by violence. Just before the actual moment of death, as the "snapping of the silken threads" begins, one will be conscious of the etheric presences of one's nearest and dearest who are due to assume charge of him. One will see and hear them in their spiritual presences as they surround him, waiting to accomplish his freedom from bodily imprisonment. He will greet them, and thereby acknowledge that they are perceived; and when the instant of complete letting-go comes, they will take charge of him. They will take charge of his Pattern Body when it exits from its lifelong enhousement.

Pattern Body is the sum and substance of all that one has been in flesh, brought up into a sublimated form. It is the individual in his *spiritualized* form, with organs and organic functions subtracted: all but the mind. That person is thinking with his spirit; he has always been thinking with the Spirit: nevertheless, Mind never quits the Pattern Body, for the Pattern Body is the soul's vehicle for exercise until Mind can think of itself without requiring a physical or illuminatory vehicle to identify itself.

When the Light Body or atomic Pattern Body releases its magnetic clutch on the sequestered atoms and permits them to fall away from it, disintegration of the Atomic Structure results because the Spirit-Soul, or the Self-Recognizing Thought Unit, withdraws the Light Pattern Body from its enhousement of atoms.

When the body gives up its "ghost" or becomes Etheric, the pineal and pituitary glands give up their domination over the rest of the human frame and let it lie in a comatose and disintegrating form of manifestation which is sometimes suspended animation, but more often physical death.

The Light Pattern Body continues in existence: It is the Form that Self-Recognizing Consciousness keeps around itself to give visual identity to others on higher etheric planes. It can, and eventually does, discard such Light Pattern Body when its purpose and function has been served.

The Pattern Body is what the discarnate friends take in their charge, in this manner: They recall a sense of the mission the individual had planned for himself while on earth; then they give him a sense of astral happenings on the Thought Planes. They tell what his obligations have been to himself and to others who were recently in physical life with him. Then, they give stimulants of thought-impulses to guide him back to a sense of his etheric self by guiding him back to a sense of his *spiritual* obligations. One has particular spiritual obligations all of his mortal days: they have never been apart, even for an instant. They have always and forever "identified him to himself" every moment of his waking days in physicality. These obligations guide him even more to a sense of himself, after he hears himself summoned to these higher recognitions by his nearest and dearest. However, at first they let him "sleep"; they let him perform onto himself until he gets over the shock of the eventualities he must face, *which is squaring his current accounts with his own spiritual destiny, as he envisioned it, before he entered physical life.*

15. WHAT ARE THE SPHERES

There are etheric planes or octaves that are divided into spheres or realms. They have been given numbers ranging from the first, which is the lowest, up to the seventh, the highest. The spheres of the etheric world are ranged in a series of bands forming a number of concentric circles around the earth. These circles reach out into the infinity of space, and are invisibly linked with the earth-world in its lesser rotation upon its axis, and its greater revolution around the sun. The sun has no influence upon the ether world. The low Realms of Darkness are situated close to the earth-plane and interpenetrate it at *their* lowest.

Consciousness is a degree of planes. The History of Consciousness proceeds from the disciplines of this material earth world, up through the various etheric octaves to the State of Timelessness and Changelessness that is union of a sort with The Divine. Here are the Seven Octaves, listed in the order of their progression:

FIRST---The materialistic earthly octave where Holy Spirit has projected and crystallized atomic substances so that they control and discipline the Soul in its organic vehicle and thus educate it to think in terms of picture images derived from substance in form;

SECOND---The plane most closely enwrapping the earth is the Astral or Purgatorial octave: it is the great

Plane of Darkness or Shadow, the first step in orienting one to etheric freedom. It is the state of *add interim* affairs where ex-mortals are learning to use their spiritual perception. It is where the soul learns what it means to operate in the etheric body. Many who find themselves staying there are overly grief-stricken which serves as an anchor holding them close to the first Earth Plane.

Nothing is going to damage them. They must realize that it is best to move on, *thinking* of the dearest and kindest ones that have gone on ahead of them and asking for guidance out of that region. Thousands are borne upward through it in a comatose condition after quitting physical body, by the etheric arms of loved ones, to be summoned to the well-lighted areas of the--

THIRD---The Octave of Thought-projection. The third plane is called the Plane of Largess. It is the first reasonably well-lighted plane where the great mass of earthly people, not very good and not very bad, find themselves with their ordinary earth-lives terminated. Such people have never had much instruction in spiritual matters. They have taken earth life as they found it, lacking the curiosity to do much wondering about how they ever got into it, and being generally considered minors in any knowledge of the Eternal Verities. For the time being they are in no position to aspire any higher, or handle themselves on Planes four, five, six or seven.

The ex-mortal is achieving its first lessons in creative form in its own right. This octave is sometimes called the Octave of Illusion, though not necessarily hallucination, since what is thus created by Thought Creation can be perceived by other persons in similar states. The Soul on the Third Plane can create etherically for itself whatsoever it may fancy, *but the durability of what is created or projected depends on the strength of the Thought Force exercised to get it.*

The Rose Halls of Rest: There are Homes of Rest for those who have come upon this Higher Octave after long illness, or who have died a violent passing and who are in consequence suffering from shock. These homes are built in the classic style, two or three stories in height and are entirely open on all sides, with no windows. They are white in color as far as the materials of composition are concerned, and immediately above is a great shaft of blue light descending upon and enveloping the whole building with its radiance, the effect of which is to give a striking blue tinge to the whole edifice.

This great ray is the Downpouring of Life---a healing ray---sent to those who have already passed but who are not yet awake. When they are wholly restored to spiritual health, there will be a splendid awakening and they will be introduced to their new existence.

An outer vestibule leads into a lofty hall of considerable dimensions. The space that would ordinarily be devoted to windows is occupied by tall pillars set some distance apart, and this arrangement is carried out on all four walls. The floor is carpeted by soft covering and here and there a tapestry hangs upon its walls. Filling the whole prospect of the floor space are comfortable cots or couches, each of which hold a recumbent form, quite still, and sleeping profoundly. Moving quietly about are a number of men and women intent on watching the different sleepers. The sleepers are under the influence of the Blue Ray, and its effect is one of pronounced energizing merged with tranquility.

Relatives and friends of those who are undergoing treatment within the Halls of Rest are an important part of the awakening process. They wait close at hand for the moment of awakening. Those in attendance on the sleepers do so as though each is performing a personal labor of love, for the sheer joy of doing it. The glad awakening of each sleeping soul is an everlasting joy to them, no less than to the people who are called to meet face-to-face and voice-to-voice again with those they have long since parted from, down upon the earth plane. Following the third octave of thought projection is the---

FOURTH---An octave of increased expansion of Consciousness, the state of being where the Soul knows form in its perfection or sublimation. This is the great plane or level widely called Summerland or *The Plane of Idealized Form*, where form exists in idealty and conditions are well-nigh Utopian, causing so many to conclude they have attained the true celestial state---but by no means have they done so.

We have been many generations coming along up the Cosmic Way with a given clique or combination of individuals with whom we have gone in and out of many lives. This integration of many personalities did not happen by chance. We were cosmically inter-related generation after generation, and passing through a commonality has furnished us with a commonality of consciousness that is a distinct thing from the commonality of consciousness of all other groups we have touched or bypassed along the way. This integration and interrelation of groups is truly a fearsomely significant thing. We have thought of these intimates as having been of chance meeting and professional relationships. All the while they were members of our private cosmic group, just as distinctive in relationship to all other groups as any individual member in it. All the persons with whom we have ever had intimate relationships or Karmic debt of a personal nature or all those persons who have come along the same route of experience with us are all units in a distinctive coagulation of soul-spirits that go in and out of mortal sequences with us, all contributing to a Group Intelligence, that eventually will take on a "personality" of its own. We shall belong to it as units, as we have always belonged to it as units.

Plane Four is the Octave of Perfected Form and Color, meaning that it is the level of consciousness where all those who have mastered the Thought Technique of Plane Three come into an ideal world of etheric stability and endurance and live the very acme of the life started long before on *this* level of materiality. Anything mind can conceive in patterns of Love, Durability and Utility can reside in a permanent reality. It's a placid period of content in which one need make no exertion but live imaginatively with relatives and intimate friends and is given the soul to surfeit, existing therefore in the conditions that prevail in the Abode of the Blessed. There is neither erosion nor corruption on this plane, because the plane isn't made of earthly materials. Even buildings and landscapes projected by adept Mass Thought have beauty and performance that is "out of this world"---but it is a paradise providing for joy---*not* for evolution. The soul has experienced incarnation in Matter but has by no means come out of it as perfected as it imagined. One may find it highly desirable to return into earth-life again and again to clear up its spirit-group obligations or acquire a greater mastery over Self. This fourth plane is the octave where such deficiencies evidence themselves. The soul can come to realize that by no means is it qualified for pushing higher into the fifth plane so, after a lengthy period in Ideality of all earthly concepts, it may descend into flesh again and again to strengthen its deficiencies. Reincarnations from the Plane of Idealized Form usually have the utmost intelligence and purpose behind them.

Following this octave of Perfected Form and Color is the---

FIFTH---Cosmic Limitation of Consciousness. The soul is once more confined within a body that exists in the visible universe but detaches itself from intimate communion with its Group, assumes a body that at times seems flame-like and experiences almost stellar incarnation.

Up the Fifth Plane of Consciousness and afterwards one possesses a consciousness, not alone of what it has gone through itself, but what the members of its Group have gone through in totality. It is Consciousness operating in a different phase or aspect from what is commonly exercised on the earth plane. It is something grown toward and into, in life's higher echelons, and one gradually comes to exhaust the experience-profits in strict individuality. Following the fifth octave of Cosmic Limitation of Consciousness is the---

SIXTH---Another cosmic expansion of Consciousness in which the Soul completes its stellar experiences, *returns* to its Group Soul and holds within its consciousness awareness of the whole universe. It can still withdraw and be the traveler---one discarnate being---or it can be the one cosmic being realizing all the experiences of the group soul and through it, envision the universe.

On gaining up to the sixth plane, one reaches a condition where consciousness need no longer be identified, either by vehicle or personality but by overshadowing ability to contain all intellectuality that exists within the group. And in such state of consciousness, it is no longer required to confine one's self to forms of Matter to get expression. One of the greatest forms of expression is manifesting in, and through, Fire. It is one of the extraordinary forms and phases which consciousness can take. In "stellar" aspects, one finds one's self in such Group

Consciousness: no longer tied to our particular solar system. It is possible to move intelligently out among other star systems and constellations and know worlds beyond ours. Lastly comes the---

SEVENTH---The Plane of Infinite Expansion of Consciousness, where almost literally the traveler in Eternity becomes one with his Creator. He holds the universe within his consciousness. He is God and yet he is but one of the Many in One. In the Sixth and Seventh Plane of Expansion there seems to be little further contact with the first Earth Plane. Few souls from the Sixth or Seventh Octaves have communication with the literalities of Earth, having attained to a state which theology describes as "The Host of Just Men Made Perfect". The solar ages of such highly attained Spirits may run to millions of years.

The Seventh Plane might be described as the passage from form into formlessness. The Soul has no need to express itself in shape, however tenuous, however fine. On the Seventh Plane there is a fusion with similar spirits of the cosmic group Oversoul or Mass Soul. All of it is but preparation for absorption into the Godhead---which happens on the stupendous Planes of Timelessness when the Mass Soul becomes part of the Divine Principle. The soul who enters that Seventh state passes into The Beyond and becomes One with God.

Definitions:

Ad Interim: In the meantime.
Affinity: A natural liking for someone or something.

Banality: to the point of being predictable.

Benefactor: One who gives help or money to a person or cause.

Bombastic: High sounding, but with little meaning.

Celerity: Swiftness of movement.

Circumscribe: To restrict something within limits.

Compendium: collection of information about a particular subject.

Congenital: Especially of disease. Habit or abnormality from birth.

Caprice: Tendency for sudden or unpredictable change.

Counterpoint: To emphasize by contrast.

Declension: A condition of decline.

Dissolution: Closing down or dismissal of an assembly, partnership or official body. Dissipation.

Discernment: To judge well.

Elucidations: Explanation to make clear.

Erroneous: Wrong, incorrect.

Evince: Show itself, demonstrate or manifest.

Exactions: The act of demanding and obtaining something, especially a payment or service.

Facile: Oversimplification.

Fecund: Capable to produce an abundance of offspring.

Flagrant: A wrong obviously offensive.

Hoary: So aged as to inspire great respect, Ancient.

Idealized: Perfect, or better than reality.

Immutable: Unable to be changed.

Inane: Silly, stupid or foolish, senseless, frivolous.

Inertly: A state of slow motion. Moving or acting slowly.

Inimical: Tending to harm; hostile.

Inexorably: Not able to be stopped or changed.

Iniquity: Immoral or unfair behavior, sin, wickedness.

Insensible: Unable to feel or perceive. Unconscious.

Interminable: Incapable of being terminated.

Irascible: Easily angered.

Maudlin-Overly emotional or sentimental.

Malice: Wrongful intention.

Postulate: A thing assumed to be true as the basis for reasoning.

Proclivities: An inclination toward a particular thing.

Providence: The protective care of God.

Purblind: Impaired or defective vision, slow or unable to understand.

Quiescent: A state or period of inactivity or dormancy.

Rebuff: To reject ingraciously.

Recalcitrant: Obstinately uncooperative attitude.

Resolute: Purposeful and determined.

Resplendent: Attractive and impressive through being richly colorful or sumptuous.

Requisition: To formally demand performance of.

Sacrosanct: Too valuable or important to be interfered with.

Sentient: Able to perceive or feel.

Solicitude: Above average care or concern for someone or something.

Subjectivity: Personal perspective and perceptions versus outside influence.

Sublimated: Greatness beyond measure.

Surfeit: To feed or supply to excess.

Tenuous: Very weak or slight.

Unilaterally: One sided.

Printed in Great Britain
by Amazon

80178895R00047